WHY I SURVIVED

WHY I SURVIVED

Where Survival Becomes Strength

Jennifer Lee

Why I Survived: Where Survival Becomes Strength

Published by Jennifer Lee

Second edition

Printed in the United States of America.

Paperback ISBN: 979–8-9873321-4-6

Note: At the time this book was originally published, the accompanying podcast was titled *I Need Blue*. In 2026, the podcast was renamed *The Healing In Sharing podcast.*

PRAISE FOR
WHY I SURVIVED

Maria Z.

***5.0 out of 5 stars* Concise and heartfelt**

Reviewed in the United States on October 30, 2024

This book taught me a great deal about victimization, especially of someone who because of their empathy and kindness, made for an easy target by unscrupulous people. The author, Jennifer Lee, describes repeated traumas by such people in a clear, concise, yet compassionate narrative. She doesn't write out of self pity or revenge, but to offer an invitation to other trauma survivors as well as those who have no experience with the sinister motives that people can present. Dating abuse was a term new to me, however, being a parent, I now identify it well. Jennifer Lee is provides hope and strength for those seeking safety and relief by sharing her stories of incredible empathy to self-doubt to realization and empowerment. Her journey is an amazing one as she continues helping survivors through podcasts and in her community. I highly recommend this book.

M. Lauer

***5.0 out of 5 stars* We are Stronger Than We Know!**

Reviewed in the United States on October 20, 2023

This is an amazing story of resilience and perseverance to overcome and be able to heal. It was so difficult to read about what happened to Kristin, but her story is well told. To know her and see how strong she has become is incredible. I highly recommend this book, but be prepared for heart wrenching parts.

Tiffany B

***5.0 out of 5 stars* A Riveting Collection**

Reviewed in the United States on October 21, 2023

This is an inspirational collection of real-life stories that will keep you on the edge of your seat. Employing grace, honesty and candor, the author shares experiences that impacted her life as well as her insights as a survivor. I recommend this collection to anyone who has experienced trauma and is seeking a way forward.

Amazon Customer

***5.0 out of 5 stars* Real, raw & enlightening!**

Reviewed in the United States on March 21, 2023

Jen Lee is amazing! She was real and raw in her expression of her experiences. I read the entire book in one hour; I couldn't put it down. I will be sharing this book with others who I believe can use Jen's openness to help heal their own traumas!!! I love you, Jen Lee!!

RESOURCES FOR DATING ABUSE

The National Domestic Violence hotline: 800–799–7233

LEARN MORE ABOUT *THE HEALING IN SHARING* PODCAST

Website: TheHealingInSharing.com

YouTube: @TheHealingInSharing11

Facebook: @TheHealingInSharing

Instagram: @TheHealingInSharing

The Healing In Sharing podcast is available on Apple Podcasts, Spotify, and most other listening platforms. Subscribe today!

QUESTIONS OR COMMENTS

Email: TheHealingInSharing@gmail.com

DEDICATION

This book is dedicated to what *is* inside you:
resilience, strength, courage, hope, perseverance, and love!

TABLE OF CONTENTS

PROLOGUE

My hand was on the refrigerator door, getting ready to pull it open, when I heard this fierce inner voice say, "It's time to share your story."

But I'd never discussed the robbery and abduction outside of court before. People knew it had occurred, after all, it was big news in the local paper, but it wasn't a topic others brought up.

Yet at that moment, the thought of sharing my story lit a fire inside me that could have melted every piece of ice in the freezer.

That fire still exists.

That calling, which led me to become the creator and host of the *I Need Blue* podcast, began in April 2021. I knew nothing about podcasts; I didn't even listen to them. However, taking on a challenge to help others was right up my alley. Now in season three, *I Need Blue* continues to create a space where survivors of life events feel they belong, are loved and understood, and, my favorite, empowered!

As I reached out into my community, I found others who had experienced a traumatic event or knew someone who had. No one is immune to the devastating effects of living with trauma, whether from a violent crime, an abusive relationship, addiction/recovery, human trafficking, or many other situations less often discussed. I realized there was a need to share and expose the realities of people's experiences. And the more present I became in my community, the more people wanted to share.

And the *I Need Blue* podcast was born.

MY STORIES

Why I Survived is my story, a memoir. It reflects my current recollections of life experiences. I recognize that others' memories of the events described in this book may differ from my own. Some names and identifying details have been changed to protect the individuals' privacy, as this book is not intended to harm anyone. Some events have been compressed, and some dialogue has been recreated.

Story 1: As you read my story, you will see that the abuse I endured was not physical but mental and emotional. It was slow and subtle. Not all trauma is linked to a violent crime. This experience has been my secret until now. For the first time, I am ready to share my story of surviving an abusive relationship.

Story 2: My story of surviving an armed robbery and abduction is well known to most, and it is the topic I share when asked to guest speak at different venues.

Story 3: Early in 2022, someone forced their way into my space. I felt an immediate surge of fear, just as I had during the robbery. Listening to my gut and staying aware of my surroundings have led me to focus on situational awareness.

Story 4: This is an inspirational story in which I learned the difference between our intentions and our purpose and how overcoming fear can help us help others. I'm excited to share it with you!

This book is for those seeking validation and for understanding that it is OK to share their truth. It is a resource that offers tools to support someone in their healing process. This book is not for those who judge or question anyone's experience, emotions, or reactions. The content is not for everyone, and that is OK.

TRIGGER WARNING

PLEASE NOTE: This book contains stories with graphic themes, including violence, abuse, and terror, and may not be suitable for all readers.

Some topics may be triggering.

Please seek help if needed.

Remember, you always come first!

YOU ARE

stronger

THAN YOU

THINK

STORY 1

DATING ABUSE IS SLOW AND SUBTLE

AUGUST 2003

Like most weekdays, this day had been a long one selling cars. Being a car salesperson was an interesting job, working most weekends and being part of the infamous group of people standing "on point," waiting for the next car-buying victim.

I'd left my retail position thinking commission was a better gig, but for me, it wasn't. I was poor and barely able to pay rent. While I could demo our brand, the trick to selling cars was understanding all brands. I lacked the general passion for cars that would motivate me to learn about them. As the months went on, it became clear I would have to find another way to pay my bills.

One obvious solution was to get a roommate. Thankfully, the front office at my apartment complex found a roommate for me: a woman named Kim!

Life was stabilizing. A job and a new roommate were on the way, both giving me the ability to pay my bills. At that moment, Rob entered my world. I was in the bar of a Mexican restaurant, having a margarita with a friend, when a man walked in. The restaurant was dimly lit, and the smell of homemade chips and spicy salsa hung in the air. Even in that light, I could tell he was dressed in a nice suit and didn't seem to belong there. He was different, and I found that intriguing.

I looked at my friend Joe and said, "I think I need to say hi to him." So, with my ultra-confident personality, I walked over to this man and introduced myself.

We talked for a couple of minutes, then I returned to Joe and filled him in on the details. The man's name was Rob. He was in town on business; he lived in New Jersey and worked in New York; he didn't have kids and wasn't married. After Joe and I finished our drinks, we headed our separate ways. On the way out, I walked over to Rob to say goodbye and thank him for the conversation. I wished him safe travels home and left the restaurant, knowing I'd never see him again.

The next day, I took a break during a slow spell at work and left with one of my coworkers to look at furniture for her new apartment.

When I got back, my colleagues told me a guy named Rob had stopped by to say goodbye. He'd left his phone number. I was flattered and surprised. Apparently, I'd made a positive impression on him. Since he'd gone out of his way to find me, I thought the least I could do was call to say thank you. I left a message thanking him for stopping by and saying I was sorry I'd missed him. I was sure he'd gone back to the hustle and bustle of his big-city life, and I continued to spend my weekends at the dealership. I lasted a few more months, then left the car business and headed back to retail.

OCTOBER 2003

Two months later, Rob called to say he would be in town for his birthday at the end of December and wanted to spend it with me. Once again, I felt flattered and readily accepted his invitation.

NOVEMBER 2003

By November, Rob and I were having daily phone calls, often multiple times a day. Many of them began with "You are my sunshine, and I just needed to hear your voice," or something equally romantic. I found him dreamy.

He would ask me about my day, and I would always explain in detail. "It was great. I met my store sales goal." Or, "There was a crazy customer today." Or, "Someone tried to return a visibly used item."

He would ask me what I was doing, and sometimes I'd answer, "I'm going out with my friend for a drink or dinner." Rob would ask, "Which friend? Have you known them long? Where are you going? Text me when you get home."

By then, he'd become part of my world, so sharing my day felt natural. I'd ask him about his day, and the answer was usually the same: stressful. He kept busy in the evenings. Between karate, playing cards, and hanging out with friends, we couldn't talk much on most nights. I worked in retail management, so I often started early and stayed late.

DECEMBER 2003

I was working as an assistant manager at a body lotion store, and the holidays were upon us! We sold lotions, massage oils, candles, kitchen soap, and a new line of men's products. The holidays were always buzzing with new products and excitement. But I also had other reasons for feeling this excitement and energy: Rob would be arriving soon!

When he arrived in town, he drove straight to the store to meet me. He walked through the door wearing a tan Versace suit. He was taller than me, with a bit of a gut, and he spoke with a New York accent, carrying himself with confidence and finesse. He spoke proper English and was a graduate of the

University of Massachusetts. Again, I was drawn in by how different he was from everyone else I knew.

I introduced him to my manager before heading to dinner. He told me to pick the restaurant. He intimidated me, even over small things like choosing a restaurant. But I chose the local steakhouse, Lonestar. I figured there was nothing like a great steak and potatoes! He may have been used to finer dining. I wasn't worldly, and I assumed I didn't match what he was used to in women. But for some reason, I was the woman he picked, and we were celebrating his birthday.

Dinner was great, and the conversation never stopped. We had already talked many times by then, but I always learned something new in each conversation. We talked about our future. He stayed for the weekend, then headed back to New Jersey. The year 2004 was around the corner, and it was starting with a new relationship. I had butterflies in my stomach thinking about Rob, and he treated me wonderfully. He spared no expense and always had plenty of cash on hand. He drove a green Saab with a stick shift. I never had to worry about driving. Even though I had previously sold cars, I only knew how to drive an automatic.

JANUARY 2004

While I was at work, my manager said, "A package arrived for you."

I looked at my manager in surprise. "What do you mean, a package arrived?"

It was a small TV from Rob. Apparently, he liked to fall asleep watching TV at night, so he sent me this television for my bedroom. It was 19'', and it would fit on top of the small three-drawer chest I had. It would be there for him when he stayed. How thoughtful! Now I can watch TV, too. I couldn't wait to call and say thank you.

FEBRUARY 2004

Rob had a work training seminar in Chicago, and he was flying me there so I could spend the weekend with him. It was only my second time on an airplane, and I was nervous, but the anticipation of seeing him was exciting. He was kind, generous, and exciting, and I was happy to make him happy; his happiness was my happiness. He showed appreciation for and support of me, my job, and my family. It seemed too good to be true, but he had easily slipped into the role of my boyfriend.

We stayed downtown at a fancy hotel. The meals were exquisite, considering I'm "fussy" about food. Remember, meat and potatoes! Rob took me shopping and bought me some clothes. He paid cash. I wasn't used to being spoiled and the center of attention. I had never imagined I would be so blessed, and I could never thank him enough. I left on Sunday, and he stayed behind for the week to attend more meetings.

My heart flip-flopped when we talked, and I was always giddy to talk to him. By then, I had a good job, paid my bills, and rented a nice apartment I shared with my roommate. I was on a healthy, independent path, and then Rob joined me on it. But that all began to change slowly with Rob's requests.

MARCH 2004

Rob had always asked me many questions about where I was and who I was with. It seemed normal to me; however, his responses to my answers were changing. He would make me feel guilty. "Why do you want to go out with your friends? Am I not fun enough? Are you not happy? If this isn't working, we don't have to be together."

I didn't understand. We'd just spent a great time in Chicago. I was happy. He was fun. I did want us to be together, but maybe I wasn't doing enough to show it. I knew I needed to do better. So I decided to spend less time with my friends so he would be able to tell it was him I wanted.

We saw each other for four days in March. It was hard; the coming and going was overwhelming for me, especially given the new tone of our conversations. He said he grew up on Long Island and attended the University of Massachusetts. He also talked about his sister, who had a disability, but he never talked about his parents or much of anything else from his past.

I didn't yet know that anything was wrong, though. The changes were too slow and subtle to set off alarm bells. The first real awareness came during therapy. As part of my plan for healthy living, I had been attending therapy. I think everyone should go to therapy; life throws curveballs, and sometimes we need someone to help us catch them. I didn't mind talking and sharing. I wanted to learn more about myself and how to deal with life. Since my first introduction to Rob, he has been part of my therapy conversations. As time went on, my therapist asked more questions about him. One day, she asked, "What does he do? Where does he live?" I only had vague answers. I didn't know the name of the company he worked for, and I didn't have his home address. During this time, my stress in the relationship increased, and my body reacted.

By this point, I had started to fear saying the wrong thing around Rob. I didn't want to upset him. I didn't want to see how he would react if he were really upset. Would he raise his voice? Or worse? I started getting sick to my stomach, not from butterflies. Anxiety set in, and I couldn't sleep. I didn't want another sleepless night, wondering what was wrong with me, suffering as I realized I must have been a bad person.

I ended up seeing a psychiatrist who prescribed me medication for anxiety and sleep. That helped for a little while, but eventually the sleeping pill gave me nightmares, and I needed to stop taking it.

I didn't watch basketball, but Rob introduced me to March Madness. Every year, he and his buddies would go to Vegas for March Madness. Rob shared one thing about the weekend: they would invite women up to their room to watch them take off their shirts. I didn't understand it. I didn't know how they found it acceptable, and mostly I didn't know how someone who said they loved me would want to take part. The thought of him going made me sick to my stomach and anxious, but he said he wasn't doing anything wrong. He could look but not touch. (I hate that saying!)

He instilled in me a new fear of abandonment by always threatening to leave if I didn't trust him. My decisions, such as going out with friends or family, depended on his answer. He didn't always say no, but the abrupt tone of his response made it clear he disapproved. Without realizing it, I became dependent on his approval.

By then, Rob began recognizing my triggers before I did because he was the one creating them. During this time, he decided to diagnose me as codependent. I had no idea what that meant. He bought me a book and told me to read it. It was ironic because I had been as independent as could be eight months earlier. I don't know what happened, but he always had the answer.

I was in emotional turmoil, but no one had any clue. I worked at the lotion store for about a year, and I never missed a day of work. I put a smile on my face, let laughter escape my mouth, and worked as many hours as were allowed. I would occasionally ask Rob for permission to go out with my friends after work, but I never knew how he would respond.

I started binge drinking as an unhealthy coping method. My therapist would ask about my drinking, and I would reply, "I had a couple of drinks." It was more than a couple, but I didn't want to be scolded by her, too. I remember one time when I came home from work, drank until I passed out, and woke up the next morning still wearing my dress, boots, and heavy trench coat. I will never forget that night. I will never forget the dismay and disappointment I felt about myself that morning.

I knew that waking up in my clothes, hungover and craving a drink, was neither normal nor healthy. I was my own problem, though, and Rob agreed.

During that time, I wrote several poems about my journey. I preferred typing to writing by hand. Stroking my fingers across the cool computer keyboard provided solace and a safe place to share what I held deep inside, and no one would find what I wrote. Looking over my poems as I write this book, I have a hard time reading them because I feel the pain in the words. I remember the confusion and the rollercoaster of emotions. It was exhausting to live through. You will see the difference in the poems; some reflect the "good" times, and others depict the pain.

These poems are scanned, original, unedited copies, and my grammar and typing errors remain. It is my first time sharing them with anyone.

JENNIFER LEE

The door

Feb. 8, 2004

I lay in a midst of haze
It's cold, damp and dark.
A place that has become somewhat unfamiliar
Turmoil lingers
And silence surrounds.
Only the words swirling in my head and
The hurt in my heart – only I am aware.

Someone is opening my door
A door that needs to be bolted shut.
He found the key and walked inside
Completing unknowing of what lies within.

Pushing his buttons is the only way
I know how to shut that door.
Hoping he'll come out – the door shuts behind.

There lies a world of pain, confiusion and loneliness.
A world I don't want to share.
Not many have opened that door
And none have endured afterwards.

I just want to be happy
Someone who will love me for me.
I need this challenge
For I have put it off to long.

WHY I SURVIVED

-2-

He scares me – and know I know why
He walked in that door and didn't walk out.
He challenged me in the most painful way
But I understand.

I don't like to push buttons and have this need for
control. (It's a defense mechanism)
It caused the door to open
To a place I wasn't yet ready to confront.
But he knows me to well.
And hopefully, if I'm right, won't let this door close
until it's over.

As tears fall, I feel like I just lost again!!
I contemplate why I can't let go.
Why I can't let someone in.
Am I afraid thay may hurt me
Turn their back, See too much
I push them away and go on alone.

I feel like I have been whipped on the back
The wounds heal but the scars remain forever.
My scars are visible but only I know how deep they run.

I wish they would have faced me when they hurt me
I would look them straight in the eye
For through my eyes all is revealed.

-3-

How ironic, considering they are my favorite feature.

His words triggered something deep inside me.
And caused me to lose control with my words
It's gonna cost me; It always does.
Our relationship has changed – I feel it.

The direction it goes – undetermined.
I didn't want him to go there
For only I know the reaction it causes.

I feel alone again
I feel violated; compared to others.
Like my all is no longer great, only good.

I don't want to walk this road at all
But most of all,I don't want to walk it alone.
So I will shut the book and in the morning the door will be closed.
That's how it needs to be!

I'll put my walls back up.
10x's thicker.
Delude the pain with laughter and smiles.
Color my eyes and pretty my face
No one will know!

JOURNEY'S PART II

6 MONTHS LATER

Journeys are about discovery
About cufflinks (do you remember)
About pulling each other up when down
And holding onto each other for support and balance.

Journeys are about discovering the gold
At the end of the rainbow-
The light at the end of the tunnel

Embarking upon a new journey takes courage.
You never know what lies ahead on the road.
You just know, no matter what the
Roadblocks, you couldn't image
Taking this path with anyone else.

You are the light of my life.
At a time when it barely flickered
You lit my heart on fire.
For that alone I am thankful.

I am writing to tell you
Thank you for being you.
For without you,
I would ask "who"

You are truly one of a kind
In you heart, soul and mind

-2-

In your words, I find comfort.
Your arms take away all my pain.

The man inside
Is sensitive and caring, willing
On the outside- not to hide
And always daring!

His smile is bright
Like the sunshine
He's truly a sight
And thankfully he's all mine.

You can never say thank you enough
Appreciation is always important.
Our words say a lot of stuff
Saying "thank you" is merely a start.

I love our talks
All the good and "area of opportunities"
I love our walks
And of course when we tease.

I love your thoughts and
I love that you listen to mine
I love how you get impatient and
Try to keep me in line.

-3-

I Love You[redacted]
You are a part of my mind, heart, and soul
I want ot make sure you see
You light my heart on fire
As though a piece of coal.

May that coal burn always and forever!

Love,

Jen

MAY 2004

My therapist made me realize it was odd that I knew so little about Rob. I hadn't met a single friend or family member of his. I didn't even have his address! I took a risk and kept asking him where he lived. After enough questions, he invited me to his house in New Jersey. He said he lived with a roommate who wouldn't be there when I visited. It was going to be just Rob and me.

The weather was beautiful for the six-hour drive. It was dark when I arrived, but I could still see the house was brown and mostly brick. Two stories. I knocked on the door, excited to see him. This trip was going to answer some of the questions my therapist had about his identity. When he opened the door, I smiled, gave him a big hug, and told him I'd missed him. He said he'd missed me, too. But before I went inside, he asked me to park in front of the house on the other side of the street. Sometime in the middle of the night, he pulled my car into his driveway, where it was hidden from view.

His home was clean and modern inside. What I remember from walking in was a large fish tank with exotic fish swimming about. Upstairs, he showed me a bedroom and bathroom, but not the other rooms.

After the tour of his house, we went back to the living room, where he led me to the coffee table. On it sat a light-pink, crocodile-pattern Kate Spade purse. Structured. Shoulder handles. It was beautiful! I picked up the bag and saw the $400.00 price tag. "This is for me?" I asked. "Yes, beautiful. It's for you. I love you," he said. I gushed over the bag.

He knew I shopped at Goodwill. I enjoyed the hunt, and it also fit my budget. This "bag," this gift, was something different for me, something special. Instantly, I forgave him for any harsh words or negative feelings he'd left me with. We loved each other, and he'd invited me into his home. I needed to be a good girl. He deserved that.

The next day, we decided to visit the Bronx Zoo. On the way, his driving was erratic, and it scared me so badly I almost had an anxiety attack. I mentioned that he didn't drive like that when he visited me. "It's how we drive in NY," he said. I didn't like it.

We passed a billboard for Scores's new location, and he noted it with much interest in his voice. It was obvious he had visited this strip club before and wanted to go again. It made me sick to my stomach. Memories of another trauma flooded back, and I felt a familiar pain. I didn't want to be in that moment, so I started talking myself out of my bad feeling. "He invited you here. He chose you. You shouldn't feel this way. He bought you a purse, and now he's taking you to the zoo. Stop feeling this way." I was on a downward spiral and fighting it. Two anxiety pills later, I started to feel better.

On the second day, we headed downtown. We took the subway, transferring from one train to another. I would have been lost without him. When we reached our destination, we found a store with a garage door at the front. The prices were great, and I was looking around at all it had to offer when, suddenly, the garage door closed. I'd never experienced anything like it. I later learned that stores like that pull down their doors when they're afraid they're about to be raided.

The garage door lifted after just a few minutes, and we were back on our way. Then we went to a market area (I realized later it was a black market, probably selling stolen goods). I bought a wallet for my new purse, a magnet, a picture frame, and a few other trinkets. I had a slice of NY pizza, folding it to create a ditch for the grease to collect. It was so good! I had a great time, but on the way home, his mood darkened. He looked at me and said, "You weren't as excited to see New York as I thought you would be." I said, "I've seen New York on TV, so I kind of knew what to expect," but I couldn't shake the feeling that I'd disappointed him.

We had talked about going to a club that evening, so he'd taken me shopping and had me try on dresses that weren't necessarily my style. I liked to be more covered than his tastes seemed to run. As I was putting on one last dress in the fitting room, I remembered his comment about Scores, and I didn't feel right. I told him I wasn't feeling well, so we headed back to his place. We got on the subway, and I laid my head on his shoulder. I was tired. So tired and sluggish. Later, when we sat down to dinner, I remember sliding down, out of my chair, onto the floor. We didn't go out that night; instead, he put me to bed. At least that's what I think happened: I don't remember going to bed, just waking up in it. It was as though I had passed out or something. This "passing out" happened a few times during our relationship, and looking back, I think he may have drugged me.

When I awoke, Rob wasn't lying next to me. It was early morning, and he was nowhere to be found as I headed downstairs. His car was gone, and a note said he would be back in forty-five minutes. I called him, and he said he was on his way home after picking up the dog from the kennel and would be there shortly. He never said he had a dog. That was weird!

My instincts kicked into overdrive. Something was not right! I started my search. I opened closets, drawers, the refrigerator, the file cabinet, anything to kill this intense nagging inside. I took a breath and opened the top drawer. I touched the paper edges of the colorful folders and plastic tabs, reading each one to see what piqued my curiosity. I started in the back and worked my way toward the files closest to me.

I stopped breathing. "Marriage certificate," the plastic tab read. It was a blue hanging folder. "Breathe and read," I told myself. I read his name and a woman's name on the certificate. They had been married for eight years. I didn't move. Was *this* real? Was this *their* house? Had I just slept in *their* bed? Had I sat in *her* seat in the car? Where is *she* now? I ran through the house looking for any signs of a woman living there. Clothes, makeup, Tampax, anything. Nothing!

I packed my bag as quickly as I could. I needed to be gone before he got back. I left the marriage certificate out and took the Kate Spade purse. Shaking, I got in my car and headed to the gas station. Once I was on the highway and far enough away, I called him. Before I could say anything, he said, "I'm almost home."

I said shakily, "I'm gone. I left, and you forgot to tell me you're married." I was pissed, and ironically, I felt strong. I felt my instincts were validated.

"Please let me explain," he cried, speaking at the same time. "I love you. I love you. Please hear me out. Yes, I'm married, but she's in a psychiatric ward. I had to go there this morning because she was having an episode. We might be married, but we haven't been together for a few years. She's sick. I filed for divorce, but she can't sign until she's well enough. We will be divorced."

"You're upset because I caught you," I said. Given how he made me feel over the past couple of months, I wondered whether *he* was the cause of his wife's mental illness. Did he drive her crazy?

I broke up with him and blocked his number, but it didn't end there.

JUNE 2004

I was trying to process the betrayal. I felt relief, but also a sense that I owed him the chance to explain. A broken heart is hard; an abused heart is something else. You are made to doubt your thoughts and feelings, even when the proof is right in front of you. You believe you will not find anyone else, or at the very least, anyone as good as the abuser. They have a way of stripping you of your identity; you become *an* identity. You are who they want you to be. Most of the time, I was a rag doll, thrown in the corner, tattered and longing for love. I received love only when he decided I deserved it.

So here I was, knowing he had lied and mistreated me, yet I found myself justifying it: at least they weren't acting like a married couple. Maybe she was sick, and he was obligated to check on her? He would be the spouse with the legal right to receive updates. I reminded myself that there were no signs of a woman when I stayed with him. I found myself listing everything he had done for me. By the end of June, I unblocked his number and listened to his explanation for why he hadn't told me about his wife. "I wanted to, but legally I couldn't for medical reasons. She means nothing to me. I don't love her. I love you!" he said over and over.

JULY 2004

"I can't live without you. I'm going to find a job there so we can be together. We will finally live together, and the long distance will be over. I want to make this up to you," he said. I'm reasoning in my mind: OK, he's going to move, change careers, and build a life with you; therefore, he must love you and want to be with you. You must forgive him. Remember the good times and move past the bad. We will make even better new times.

He told me he was coming to visit me next week. He missed me. Not being able to talk daily and the thought of losing me made him want to be a better man. "I have no more lies, and it feels good not to keep that from you," he said when he walked through the door for the weekend. Our relationship felt renewed. My drinking subsided, and my anxiety eased. My therapist recommended that I go in cautiously. She was right.

Things were exceptionally good for a while, but then the verbal abuse started again. He liked to target my body. One day, he looked at me and said, "You won't need implants, but you will need a breast lift one day." I haven't forgotten those words.

SEPTEMBER 2004

Rob would visit, and we didn't always have sex. I remember a male friend telling me insistently, "If he hasn't seen you in a few weeks and still doesn't want to have sex with you, he's cheating." I wasn't going to allow myself to think that. He was just tired, or maybe I made him mad? Perhaps he was punishing me? It must be my fault.

After the Low Period

September 26, 2004

I so badly want you to hold me
Just touch me
Reassure me
Tell me everything will be "OK"

There is a distance that lingers
After harsh words
Words that are hurtful
Filled with confusion

I just want to go back the happy times
When there were hugs and cuddling.
Now I feel like I'm punished.

I expect too much
After my rampage
I need to much
After I've caused damage.

It leaves me feeling sad
Like I deserve to be the trash taken out.
I so badly need to be loved, needed, and cared about
At this time.
But I have no rite to ask.

-2-

I feel like I don't deserve to be loved
And I find reasons why I shouldn't be
I search for things
Lingering on any false clue I find.

I want this to stop
I don't want to be this way
I don't want to cause pain
And I don't want to feel pain.

When this happens
I do exactly that
I feel the pain I cause
And I can't make it go away.
It just piles up.

I feel pressure
And a sense of urgency to fix this.
For if I don't
I will lose someone valuable.

I ask why me – why now
And I don't know the answer.
For in the beginning the relationship scared me
He was getting to close to fast.

WHY I SURVIVED

Now he's even closer
And it's harder for me to hide
It scares me a lot
For he has figured me out (even before I did)

I'm scared because I don't want to be like her
For I know how that ended.

His biggest concern is that it will end up that way
And I'll be alone
And he'll go on – knowing he didn't make the same mistake twice

I take pride in being different
I want my our footprints
I don't want to fit in anyone else's
I feel the pressure.

I think I have a trust issue
But more so and issue of deserving to be loved
And not being abandoned
I know how it feels to need the people you trust and love most and not have them there.
This is my greatest fear.

So now I go back in there
With the same feelings.
I need him to reach out
But I would never ask - for I don't seserve that.
Just like he didn't deserve what I did to hom

It's the cycle of my life right now
And I don't know how to make it stop.
I want off the ride
I want to feel happy, secure and loved
An it need to start with me.
I'm afraid,really afraid to embark on this
Journey because of what I might lose along the way
Bur I now I need to face the past, prtsent and future to get better.
And hope that when I reach the end-
The "pot of gold" is still there waiting for me.

**In reference to the above poem: this was an intense time. I now see that the guilt I felt about my own feelings was irrational. "I didn't want to be like *her,* his wife." I didn't want to be crazy and end up alone without *this* man.

The "false clues" are the ways I doubted myself. I needed to listen to my instincts! They don't lie. He had made me feel unworthy.

I'm glad I wrote these poems long ago. As sad as it is to read them now, I'm a stronger person because of them. This relationship didn't kill me, and I'm here today to share my message: you are not alone, and you are stronger than you think!

After this, you'll find there aren't any more writings until the end. My mind was clogged, and I couldn't put what I was feeling into words.

NOVEMBER 2004

It was my birthday month! Rob was in town and at the apartment with my roommate and me. We were taking shots of Jägermeister. Just like six months earlier, when I visited Rob at his house in New York, I got very groggy very quickly. At the time, I thought it was the alcohol, even though I'd had much more in the past and had never felt this way.

Eventually, Rob and Kim tucked me into my bed. I had trusted my roommate, but that night was different. As they left the room, I said, "Please don't sleep with him." I passed out and didn't wake until the next morning. Rob was next to me.

Nothing was said; everything seemed normal. I didn't feel groggy, just well rested. I never asked Kim about sleeping with my boyfriend. I didn't want to know. Instead, I internalized this suspicion, and it took the form of anxiety. This relationship was making me sick, yet I still believed I would be sicker without Rob.

DECEMBER 2004

For our first Christmas, Rob was with me on Christmas Eve but had to leave early the next morning to visit his family in Virginia Beach. I wasn't invited, but he consoled me with a Return to Tiffany heart necklace. I remember the trademark robin's-egg-blue box. I wore it every day until a year later, when it began to tarnish. This year, we didn't celebrate his birthday or New Year's.

JANUARY 2005

The lotion store manager and I made it through the holidays, and then she was transferred to another store. I took over as acting store manager. I attended conference calls, exceeded sales goals, and hired and trained employees. When the district manager visited, my store wasn't on the list of stores with employee vacancies. She said, "Congratulations!"

I said, "Well, we don't have a store manager. I've been filling in." She looked shocked! After successfully running the store for three months, I applied for the position but was denied the promotion. "Not enough global awareness," I was told. Whatever that means!

After being denied the promotion, I decided to try sales again and resigned. This time, I sold radio advertising instead of cars. The environment was filled with community events to attend and friendly people. The pay and perks allowed me to pay my bills and survive.

By then, it had been sixteen months since Rob and I first met at the Mexican restaurant. The phone calls and texts were happening regularly. With each visit, it was getting harder for me to say goodbye. It felt like a roller coaster. When Rob was here, everything seemed perfect, but when he was away, we argued, and everything was always my fault.

MARCH 2005

I spent the two months leading up to March Madness trying to process what Rob had told me. All the while, I tried to convince myself that my feelings were just an overreaction. After all, Rob loved me. But he was busy with his friends that weekend, and we barely spoke while he was in Vegas. He told me, "I'm not cheating. There's nothing wrong with looking." Yet I cried the whole time he was gone. I was impatient, and my thoughts were out of control. I couldn't wait for the weekend to be over!

MAY 2005

My favorite cousin was getting married in Ohio, and Rob agreed we could go. On a previous trip, he'd brought some clothes and left them in my closet. I enjoyed seeing them hanging there; I thought of it as a sign of our future. One day, he asked me to grab a white dress shirt for him to wear with his suit. No problem! As I looked in my closet, I noticed he had significantly fewer clothes. I hadn't noticed before, and I didn't remember him taking that many.

I didn't ask about it, and we flew into Ohio as planned. I was excited because Rob would meet my family on this trip. When we arrived at our hotel room, he opened the suitcase and pulled out the shirt I had packed for him. He held it up and grew angry. "This is not a white shirt, Teresa! This is a cream color. Can you do anything right? You can't even pick out a white shirt! Now what am I going to wear?"

Startled, I walked over and looked at the shirt. "I don't think anyone will know," I said.

"I know!" he said.

A second later, I realized he had called me by Teresa's name, his wife's. I burst into tears and retreated to the bathroom. My family was calling the hotel room phone, excited to see and hug me, but I didn't answer. After a few moments, I heard knocking on the door. I didn't want to open it; I didn't want them to see my tears. I had already evaded their call, so if I didn't answer the door, I was afraid it would raise concern. They knew very little about my relationship with Rob, and when I did speak of it, I said, "Everything is great! I am happy." The abuse was a secret.

I opened it a few inches. With tears running down my cheeks and red eyes, I looked at my older sister standing there. She said, "You don't have to do this. It's OK. Come with me." The tears upset her, so she wanted to console me in private. I knew she wanted to talk to understand what had happened.

"I can't," I said. "I'll be down to see you in a few minutes."

As soon as she left, Rob said, "I guess your family doesn't like me anymore." I didn't reply. When I finally made my way to my sister's room, the atmosphere was awkward. No one knew what to say.

The wedding turned out to be a disaster for me. Rob and I were sitting at a table when a family friend made a comment Rob didn't like. He got up, scraped his chair loudly on the floor, and practically ran out the door, leaving me dumbfounded. He went out to the car and drove around, doing donuts in the parking lot and kicking up a lot of dust.

We were all in shock. I asked my mom what to do, but she had no idea. So I did the only thing I could think of and left.

I got a tongue-lashing when I got in the car. "I came here for you, and you let me be embarrassed!" My crime was that I had said nothing.

It was time to be adults, but Rob was acting like a child. He pulled out of the parking lot, kicking up gravel and squealing the tires. He was driving too fast, and I was scared. When we got back to the hotel, he gave me the silent treatment.

Anxious thoughts raced through my head as we got into bed: I must fix this. I'm a bad person. I'm going to lose him, and I can't live without him. I'm worse than his wife. I must fix this.

I gave him oral sex, and he held my head down. He had never done that before because he knew I didn't like the taste. But this time, I deserved it. I was being punished. I deserved it.

On the flight home the next day, we didn't say much, and instead I wrote on any paper I could find. Journaling was my therapy, and I had a dictionary with me to write about my feelings throughout the weekend. When we arrived back, Rob didn't stay the night; he immediately headed back to New Jersey. Once again, I felt like a rag doll, discarded and thrown in the corner, this time with my dress torn, my face dirty, and my spirit broken. I wouldn't be better until he decided to pick me up and love me again.

JUNE 2005

Back home, I decided to fry fish. How hard could it be? I had about an inch of vegetable oil in a frying pan and was heating it to a nice, hot temperature. I began putting the fish in, and the flame shot up, grease splattering everywhere and white smoke filling the kitchen. It was a fire, and I didn't know what to do. I knew I wasn't supposed to put water on hot grease, but I didn't know what the other option was. So I put water on it anyway. Beads of hot grease splattered on my hands and feet. The sprinklers went off throughout the apartment, which caused the flame to die down but left a trace of black soot on the cupboards and the ceiling above the stove.

I ran out of my apartment and knocked on my neighbors' doors to alert them to the fire. The four of us ran outside and waited for the fire department to arrive. My apartment was on the second floor, and I watched as water poured out of the seam between my apartment and the one below. It was gushing! The fire trucks and ambulance arrived, and the EMTs treated my minor burns. The firefighters tried to open the sprinkler valve door, but it was locked, which was in violation of code. As more water spilled from my apartment onto the ground, I called the apartment complex management, but got no answer. The only option left: break into the sprinkler valve room. So they did, and finally stopped the water.

My apartment was destroyed. I called my roommate to tell her what happened. She wasted no time moving out and moving on. I also called Rob to tell him what had happened. I told him I was OK, but then I remembered my pink Kate Spade purse was soaked and ruined. I knew I was going to have to throw it out. He was genuinely concerned about me and generously offered to pay Kim's portion of the rent since she wasn't moving back in with me.

The apartment below, which was empty, was also destroyed. Eventually, the apartment complex tried to sue me, but because they failed to follow the code, the settlement was minimal.

I needed a place to stay that night, which led me to the home of Joe, Sally, and Chris Jones. A close family with strong ties in the community, Joe and Sally were in their seventies and lived with their son, Chris, a cancer survivor. We'd met at church before, and I felt I could go to them for help.

They welcomed me with open arms, and this began a family relationship I can't describe, except to say, "Family doesn't always mean blood." I stayed a few days until a new apartment was ready. Childhood records, among other mementos, were destroyed. Still, we salvaged as much furniture as possible, and I moved in to begin anew. Along with this new apartment came a new family!

JULY 2005

Rob flew in for the weekend, and it was so good to see him. The fire had startled me, and I missed his presence. During the visit, he connected my computer and set up my first Hotmail account, including an email address and password. After he left, I logged in to my computer, and in the toolbar was "Adult Friend Finders." I was shocked when I clicked on it: "Find singles in your area who are looking for fun."

Rob denied knowing anything about it, but I pointed out that he was the only other person who'd been on the computer. He accused me of not trusting him.

"I pay your rent," he said. "I'm making plans to move in with you. If you don't trust me, this isn't going to work." I was afraid he would leave, so I backed down. I hated being so codependent. I told myself I needed to read the book he'd given me.

After I told him I'd found the Adult Friend Finder toolbar, he deleted his browsing history every time he finished using my computer.

AUGUST 2005

Rob officially left New York and moved into my new apartment with me. He started a new job about twenty minutes away. When he arrived, he came with his car full of clothes and not much else. His car was a two-door, so he had limited space. The rest of his stuff was in storage in New Jersey, where he said it would stay until we found a larger place to live. He received a few pieces of mail at my apartment, but not much else.

It was nice living together, waking up and going to bed at the same time. If you remember, we didn't speak much on most nights because he was so busy with various activities. But now I didn't have to wonder what he was doing or who he was with. He talked about us buying a home together, but he rarely shared details about his life.

One morning, he was on the phone behind the closed bathroom door, and he said, "I love you too." When I asked who he was talking to, he said, "No one."

SEPTEMBER 2005

A month later, he walked through the door, angry.

"What's wrong?" I asked.

"They're sending me to Texas for my job in a week, and I don't know how long," he said.

As he stomped around the apartment, I felt my heart sink. I didn't want to do long-distance again. I didn't want to worry or wonder. I felt the anxiety and tightness in my stomach. What could I say? Inside, I kept telling myself: "He moved here to be with you. He loves you. It will be OK. This will be temporary." But no matter what I told myself, I was still sad.

Before he left, I introduced him to my newly found family, the Joneses. They were special to me, and I was excited to introduce them to Rob. Rob was excited to meet them, too, and to thank them for helping me after the apartment fire. We enjoyed a home-cooked meal at their home, and Joe started a conversation with Rob. He asked Rob a question about the University of Massachusetts campus because Joe had attended there as well. Apparently, Rob gave the wrong answer, indicating he had never been on campus. Joe made a mental note of the error and tucked it away, along with a feeling that something wasn't adding up.

It's normal for "outsiders" to see the red flags. As the victim in the situation, we often can't see them. Sometimes, we don't want to see them. If we feel pressured by anyone to leave or change, it can lead us to self-isolate. The Joneses stayed close to me, and that was their way of making sure I was OK, rather than coming out and telling me to leave Rob. Rob liked them and believed he'd fooled them, too.

OCTOBER 2005

I was adjusting to being in a long-distance relationship again, this time with a two-hour time difference. Nighttime calls were even harder, and I was lucky to see Rob twice a month. It sucked, but I held on to hope. I was still in therapy during this time, and I'd mentioned couples therapy to my therapist, thinking it might help our relationship and that if my therapist met Rob, she'd see he was a good person. Let's work together to determine what he needed me to change.

She was open to the idea, but not before she asked, "So, where is he staying in Texas? Do you have an address?" I replied, "I don't know." I'd asked Rob for an address, and he'd given me an excuse I'd believed. He never gave me the address, and he had an answer for everything. He could lie as if he were telling the truth.

NOVEMBER 2005

For months, I'd mention couples therapy, but Rob always resisted, even the thought of it. I'd tell him about my visits, and of course, he'd give me a list of things to bring up during the session to help me improve.

But eventually, he agreed to go to therapy. I remember sitting on the couch in my therapist's office, watching the exchange between my boyfriend and her. She asked him why he didn't have an address in Texas to provide for me. "If you had to call 911, what address would you give?" she asked.

He said, "I don't have the address on me." He told us he'd give it to me once he got it. He never gave me the address, but I found it months later.

During the session, Rob answered every question, almost in a cocky manner. She would push, and he would push back harder. We made it through one visit, and then she told me separately that she couldn't see both of us. "It's a conflict, as you are my client," she said. She was visibly frustrated, not with me, but I think she knew he was lying and couldn't catch him in it.

DECEMBER 2005

My lease was up, so I needed to move. With Rob in Texas for an indefinite period, I needed something I could afford. The Joneses introduced me to a neighbor with a finished basement that included a kitchen, living room, and bedroom. It was comforting to have family so close by, and Sunday became a tradition of us eating Red Baron pizza together! To this day, I smile and think of them every time I see a Red Baron pizza box.

Rob came to visit for two days, and during that time, we had ongoing conversations about when he would move back. He said his job could not give him an answer. I was sad and disappointed when he left for Texas, but I was getting used to it.

JANUARY 2006

A week after Rob was gone, I turned on my computer. A screen popped up: a half-naked woman sitting on a bed. "What the . . .!" I thought. A dialogue screen appeared. I sat down, staring at what was in front of me. Disbelief! Not again! I felt sick to my stomach.

Curiosity set in, and I typed "hi" into the dialogue box.

"Hi" appeared again on my screen. She had responded. I turned off the computer, jumped out of my chair, and stared at it. I was feeling so many things, first, anger!

I called Rob and told him what I found. He denied knowing anything about it. He reminded me how he'd changed his whole life, moved there to be with me, and how he travels to visit and buys me things. "If you don't trust me, this isn't going to work. I'm not going to be accused of doing something I didn't do!" he yelled. Deep down, I knew it was him. I knew he'd chatted with this girl. He knew how to manipulate me, how to plant doubt so I'd question what I said. I didn't question what *he* would say; I questioned what *I* said, believed, or saw. I was the problem.

I told Rob I needed some time, and he wasn't happy with that answer, but I stayed strong. Maybe because he lived in Texas, it was easier for me to have time. We lived together, but only for a few days each month. He had a few articles of clothing in my closet, and that was it. Never a piece of mail. I was a secret in his world, and he was distant in mine.

Something began to change inside me. I started listening to my friends and asking myself questions. It was two and a half years into the relationship, and I'd never met a family member, roommate, or coworker. No one! He'd met all of my immediate family, attended a family wedding, and knew the Joneses and my other friends. I gave him the security he needed; I had no secrets!

The distance allowed me to grow stronger, mentally and emotionally. As I began to accept that something wasn't right, I listened more to my instincts. I felt it was time to play a game; the game of my life. I was competitive by nature; I hated to lose.

APRIL 2006

By then, it had been four months since I took some time away from the relationship. Rob was coming to town and wanted to see me. He stayed at an extended-stay hotel for the weekend because I told him I wasn't ready for him to stay with me. We went to a restaurant for dinner, and I ordered a drink called a Green Monster. It was a green drink, go figure. I went to the bathroom, and I presume that's when he drugged me for the third time. We left dinner and headed back to the hotel. I remember coming out of the elevator onto our floor, skipping down the hall as we headed to our room, and singing loudly. Another hotel guest opened their door and gave me a dirty look. Inside our room, I remember lying down on the bed, him pulling off my pants, and that's it. I remember nothing else. I woke up the next morning, and he was gone. He couldn't stay the night with me; there was somewhere else he needed to be.

At that point, I hadn't yet realized he was drugging me. I thought the Green Monster had made me pass out. During the relationship, I never would have imagined someone who loved me would hurt me that way. In 2006, there was little conversation about date drugs, except at parties. Not in a monogamous relationship!

MAY 2006

Rob and I were back to talking several times a day. The relationship felt like it was returning to "normal." I was still working at the radio station, and I'd sold a fun "remote" package to a local dentist's office that month. They had become a new client of mine and wanted the morning show to broadcast live from their location. I went to the office and met the staff. We handed out swag items and had a great time. I told Rob about the event, and he was more interested than usual. He asked many questions about who I had met and whether I'd mentioned him. "No, I didn't mention you," I replied. It was a weird question. Rob wanted to be known in my circle, except this time it would be months before I found out why.

JUNE 2006

Rob was back in town and wanted to take me somewhere special, The Jefferson Hotel, rich in history and beautiful architecture. Rob never spared any expense and always paid in cash. He was making a greater effort to reestablish our relationship and wanted to stay with me at my apartment. I told him he could the next time he came to town and handed him a key. He was thrilled.

JULY 2006

Rob walked into my apartment with his own key. I hugged him and said, "Welcome home." At the time, I was growing stronger inside, but I was still drawn to him. Something was pulling me in, as though the relationship wasn't meant to end. Then a phone call in August confirmed it.

AUGUST 2006

"I'm moving back. We will live together, and the long distance will be over. I need you to call your Realtor friend and start looking at homes!" I was so excited. Finally! I called my friend and explained the situation. I was off weekends, so we scheduled showings as soon as I could make it. My friend said he needed a preapproval letter for his funding, but Rob insisted we didn't need one because he had the money. Since the Realtor was a friend who trusted me, I was able to sidestep that step. We proceeded with the showings. Over the next couple of weeks, we reviewed ten houses, and I reported back to Rob what I found, but nothing impressed him enough to move forward.

A few weeks later, Rob said, "I'm going to have to wait until I get there." I had just wasted my friend's time and mine. One minute I was excited about getting a house together, and the next I was disappointed. This was the typical roller coaster ride. My euphoric feeling of love was dissipating, replaced by a nagging sense that something wasn't right.

Several months earlier, someone had given me the name of a local spiritual healer who read cards, so I called her and made an appointment. At that point, I was looking for someone to tell me, "Be patient with your relationship. It's going to get better." I walked into her room, introduced myself, and she immediately grabbed a bottle and sprayed the room. I thought that was odd, but OK. She shuffled the cards, dealt three piles, and told me to pick one. I didn't know which one to pick. I put my hand over the top of each pile. When I put my hand over one deck, the bottom of my hand got cold, I mean, really cold. That's the one! So I picked up the pile, and she began to read. She flipped over a card, looked at me, and said:

"The past three years of your life have been a lie, a dream, a fantasy. Nothing has been real."

I sat there, dumbfounded and in disbelief. We also talked about other topics, and she was spot on. The fact that she was right about those meant she might be right about this.

I thanked her and left with more questions than answers. I immediately called Rob and told him what she'd said. He got angry and said it wasn't true. He wanted her name and phone number so he could see her too and prove she was a fraud. I gave him the information.

After this reading, my urge to stay strong and smart intensified. I kept this feeling a secret, masking it with my obedience to him. When you're in a relationship with this kind of invisible abuse, you feel stupid. You really do. You're led to believe you make the wrong decisions, so eventually you make none. Instead, you ask for advice or permission.

I started pulling away emotionally, but I knew I wasn't meant to leave. I was meant to find answers, even if doing so could put me in danger. If his wife were still in his life and I found out, how would he react if I called him out on it? He had gone to great lengths to pull this off for three years. He wasn't just going to walk away, and I wasn't going to walk away without him paying for what he'd done to me for three years.

SEPTEMBER 2006

"I found us a house," Rob said. Wow! I didn't even know he had been looking. He said it had four bedrooms and would need some remodeling. Apparently, the kitchen ceiling needed to be redone because it was caving in. A month later, I found the house and knocked on the door. A woman answered, confirming my suspicions.

This period in our relationship was so confusing. I would pull back, and Rob would then do something on a "higher" level to lure me back in. First, he was moving back to town, and second, he'd found us a house. These were major steps forward. He was due to move back in November, and our life would begin. But not before one more visit in October.

OCTOBER 30, 2006

Rob was staying at an extended-stay hotel. He opened the hotel room door, and I walked in. Immediately, I noticed he had more items in the room than usual. Clothes were hanging in the closet. It looked like he had moved into this room rather than just staying for a few nights. It was a sign of a permanent change; he would be moving back. I felt a sense of relief that this part wasn't a lie. With him close, I could finally find answers to the nagging feeling that something wasn't right.

The next morning, Rod had left for work, and I was sound asleep when I suddenly sat up in bed and heard the words, "You need to search!" I began searching the drawers, which were full of his clothes, watches, ties, and other odd items. I opened the closet, where clothes hung, and in the back was a black duffel bag. I pulled it out and put it on the bed. It was full of pockets, and I started to unzip them one by one. Inside, I found a paper receipt from the hotel listing his residential address, and the ZIP code on that address matched the hotel's ZIP code. I wrote down the address, put the duffel bag back where I found it, and got ready for work.

I had a coworker, Casey, with whom I'd shared some things, and I told her I needed her help. She was more than willing. I gave her the address and said I'd call her that night. I needed someone to know where I was and what I was doing.

After dark, I called her, and she used MapQuest to get directions to the address on the hotel receipt I had found earlier in Rob's room. We stayed on the phone as she helped me navigate street by street. The address was only two miles from my job; this was getting too close for comfort.

I finally found the location and the house that matched the address. In the window was the big fish tank I'd seen in New Jersey. "This must be his house!" I said.

"What are you going to do?" Casey asked.

"I'm going to knock on the door!"

"But you don't know who's there? This could be very dangerous!" she said. "You found the house. You should just leave."

"I can't! I must find out!" There was no going back.

I pulled into the driveway, hung up the phone, got out of my car, and walked to the front door. I knocked and waited. The red door opened, and a woman stared at me. "Are you Teresa?" I asked.

She replied, "Yes."

I swallowed the lump in my throat. "I have been dating your husband for three years. I didn't know about you. I'm so sorry. I didn't know about you."

I was scared and sad at the same time. She looked at me and said, "I've seen your picture." She seemed so calm, but I have to imagine she felt the same shock and betrayal I did.

She opened the front door and told me to come in. I stopped after a few steps and asked, "Where's Rob? He's supposed to meet me in a couple of hours, and he's staying at a hotel down the road."

She replied, "Robert is on the other side of town playing cards." She used his full name. We were talking about the same person, but each of us called him by a different name. Teresa suggested we call him, and I agreed.

She called him, and he answered right away. "Robert, someone's here to say hi," she said.

I took the phone and said, "Hi. It's Jen." A click followed a moment of silence. He'd hung up. We called back. Voicemail. In that moment, Teresa and I weren't angry with each other, just numb. I didn't know how she'd react when she opened the door, but she deserved to know the truth. I felt a sense of relief that I was right: something was wrong, he wasn't telling me the truth, and I had just confirmed it.

Inside the home, we turned left and entered a den where I sat on the couch. I think we were both in shock. We were two women who loved the same man. We shared the same emotions of betrayal, sadness, loss, and anger, along with a swirl of others that couldn't be named. Teresa and I were connected by deceit, and the level of deceit was about to escalate in a way I never could have imagined.

Teresa decided to call Robert's mom. "Mom, it's Teresa. I have something to tell you. Robert has been seeing someone else for three years, and she's sitting next to me right now." Robert's mom hung up, too.

I stood up and asked to use the bathroom. I had to walk through the kitchen, where I stopped and looked up. The kitchen ceiling needed fixing. It looked like it was falling. Wait! Rob said the home he was buying for us needed repairs to the kitchen ceiling. This is the home Rob was talking about? This is the home he said he was buying for us? Was he moving her out and me in? I no longer had to pee.

I walked back to the den and shared my observation with Teresa. She wasn't surprised. She pointed to some apartment brochures on the fireplace mantel. She was moving out. They were having marital problems and needed time apart.

I had to ask about their sex life, and she told me they hadn't had sex in about five years. Well, at least he wasn't sleeping with both of us. But she mentioned he had pictures of other women. I didn't want to hear it.

I told her about the house I'd stayed in New Jersey, and she revealed that it was her home. During that time, she was, in fact, in a mental hospital. She'd been married to Rob for eight years, and he'd broken her down to the point where she couldn't manage her health. She had tried to commit suicide. I understood being broken down by this man. It was different for me because I was exposed to him less. She had lived with him, and he easily drowned her in his poison. He was a sick man, and we shared a mutual desire to make him pay.

I never left that night. Teresa and I talked and talked until I eventually fell asleep on the couch. I learned that Rob had a new job I didn't know about. Apparently, he'd lost his first job at the bank because he'd used their FedEx labels for personal use. At least, that's what he'd told Teresa, though I don't necessarily believe it was the truth.

He worked for a large technology company downtown, and Teresa and I decided to visit him there. We parked and walked to the security booth in the garage. We told the attendant who we were looking for and explained that Teresa was his wife and I was her friend. A minute later, the attendant told us he wasn't there. We weren't surprised.

Next, we headed to the hotel room. My key didn't work, but housekeeping was on the floor, and I persuaded them to open the door. I looked at Teresa and said, "This is where he's been staying." We took all his clothes out of the closet and laid them on the bed. We took his Rolex watches and laid them on the bed, too. We laid everything we found on the bed. On top of the stack, we left the receipt with his address. We took nothing; we weren't there to steal, but to leave a clear message. Now it was lunchtime, and we were hungry.

NOVEMBER 2006

The next day, I called the owners of the home I was renting and told them about Rob. They changed the locks. Later, I found his key lying in the driveway. He'd tried to get in. I was one step ahead in this dangerous game. For a short while, I stayed with the Joneses. I parked my car behind their house. They were understanding and always willing to help. After all, he'd lied to them, too.

I became more aware of my surroundings when I walked to and from my car. One day at work, I got a call from Rob. He was pleading with me to stop and kept saying that Teresa's dad was crazy and coming after him. I told him whatever happened to him was what he deserved. "She's crazy. You don't know Teresa as I do," he told me. He was desperate, and it was evident in his voice.

Leaving is the most dangerous part of an abusive relationship because the abuser realizes they're losing control. In Rob's case, he was losing control, and his whole world was caving in like the ceiling in his kitchen. There was no contractor to call to fix it. He'd made this mess and would have to deal with the destruction it was causing in his life. In the meantime, I needed to stay safe.

As twisted as it sounds, Teresa and I became friends. Who else could understand my emotions about this lie except the other woman who had been lied to? She knew what it was like to be in a relationship with him, including the abuse, the codependency, the porn, and the stories. She filled in the blanks for me. She knew his family, something I didn't.

Whenever I could, I gave her pictures and emails. Anything she needed to build a case against Rob. She would buy me gifts to say thank you, like clothes and meals. She was no longer working and was supported by Rob. He was still paying the bills, and now was not the time for him to stop contributing.

When they'd first moved to the area, she had a job at a dentist's office (I did find out he was using her paycheck to pay my rent after the fire. She never knew where he spent the money.) But one day, out of the blue, he told her to quit. She liked the job, and he never explained why he needed her to leave. It turned out that the dentist's office where she worked was the same one where I held the radio station event. That was why he'd asked me so many questions about that event, what a crazy, sticky web he was spinning, and what a crazy web I was unraveling!

DECEMBER 2006

I went shopping and pulled out my credit card to pay for my purchase. It was denied. I hadn't used it recently, so I knew it couldn't be maxed out. But when I called the credit card company, they told me it was maxed and listed some prior purchases. I told the representative I hadn't made those purchases, and I was eventually credited for the charges. I went to the police department, and an investigation began.

A shoe store where purchases had been made had video footage, and the cops wanted me to review it. I recognized the woman checking out with my credit card. It was Teresa! She had used my card at several stores, and some of the items she had given me were thank-you gifts. I was sick to my stomach; she was a criminal who had stolen from me. She lied, betrayed me, and fooled me, too. She was as crazy as her husband! I was mad and in quite a situation. The police needed time to gather more evidence. They were investigating larceny, identity theft, and credit card fraud. Just like with Rob, I kept up the conversation with her as if everything were normal, all the while knowing she had stolen from me and was a liar, but I played "stupid" again.

For the past three years, I had been repeatedly knocked down, but I refused to stay down. They didn't see that. They saw a naïve, kind, giving person they could manipulate. They lived in a world of "how can I benefit from this situation or this person?" They were con artists, and I felt it was time to stop them so they couldn't hurt anyone else.

Rob hadn't bothered me in weeks. After all, I had nothing left for him to take. But Teresa was a different story. I didn't tell anyone that she had taken my card. The investigation was under wraps, and I helped the investigators when needed. I started getting "busy" and talking less to Teresa. I was slowly pulling away, all the while knowing this was going to end in her arrest.

JANUARY 2007

Rob called me, freaking out! "She was arrested. What have you done?"

"I didn't do anything. She stole my card and broke the law," I said.

He pleaded with me not to press charges. I couldn't control the larceny charge; the stores were pressing charges against me. But the credit card fraud and identity theft were within my control.

MARCH 2007

I didn't want to go to court, but I didn't have a choice. Chris Jones accompanied me. I was there for fifteen minutes and never saw Teresa. I decided to drop the charges; nolle prosequi.

As I walked out of court, Chris looked over at me and said, "Boy, you know how to get yourself into some crap!" I felt like I walked around with the word "crazy" written on my forehead, a magnet for attracting people like that. At the end of the day, what did either of them gain from behaving that way? I will never know, and honestly, it doesn't matter. I did leave them with one last gift, though: my forgiveness.

I didn't press charges against Teresa. She was a victim in this, too. She had her own reasons for deceiving me, perhaps as a scorned wife. I know what she did was wrong and that she broke the law, but she was already being punished under the larceny charge. Perhaps knowing she was already facing consequences for her actions gave me room to have compassion. I haven't had any further communication with her since the arrest. The chapter on Teresa was closed!

A few months after the court proceedings, I dialed Rob's number. I prayed he wouldn't answer, and he didn't. I left this voicemail: "I'll never know why you did what you did, but I want you to know I forgive you. Even if you don't think you need my forgiveness, I forgive you." I hung up, never to dial his number again. The chapter with Rob was closed!

I found something I wrote that captured how I felt during this time. The writing is sloppy, but I wanted to share it.

A journey of 3 years has ended
No fairy tale ending
All my ~~love~~ pain I am sending
To help you w/mending

For I am alone
Like never before
Alone w/my thoughts
Why did I open the door

Because I loved you
Like no one before
There is no more to give
now I must live

The hole inside me is dark
There is no longer a spark
The warmth is gone
Feelings no longer belong

The anger has erased
It infested me like a disease
Numbness Resides
& along w/it my cries

Cries no one can fix
Its part of the mix
Ingredients of torment
Disbelief hurt & disappointment

The pain cuts like a knife
Just like the roll of the dice
You take a chance
And lose your last dance

The journey that once was
is now over ~~because~~
all because
there was another

It's hard to understand
that ~~[illegible]~~ ~~[illegible]~~ the one I loved
that man
is no longer in demand

I gave all I had
Till I got mad
Couldn't take any more
Need to shut the door.

The pain is real
It's a big deal
Want it to end
as though it never began.

The kisses + hugs
that once healed
No longer help
the ~~[illegible]~~ hand I was dealed.
shitty

I must take a different Path
And try to add up the math
~~Make the figs~~
MAKE sense of the figures
Before I wither.

I have forgiven you for what you have done
Glad I feel the most pain
& not you
I only wanted you to be happy too.

There is no happy ending
No joy & no new beginnings
That's only in fairy tales

I have little faith in Dreams
For reality is a bitch
~~[illegible] a bitch~~
Even though it seems
Life is but a dream

I hope some day I wake up!!

Facts about dating abuse and resources

Dating violence is more common than you think. One in three teens in the US will experience physical, sexual, or emotional abuse from someone they're in a relationship with, and that is just one of the sad statistics. Dating violence can take many forms, including physical violence, coercion, threats, intimidation, isolation, and emotional, sexual, or economic abuse.

The difference between domestic violence and teen dating violence is the living arrangement. In domestic violence cases, you typically live together, which makes it easier for the abuser to isolate the victim.

You may have heard people say things like, "Why would they stay if they're being abused?" or "Why don't they just leave?" These comments and questions can be hurtful and can place blame on the person experiencing the violence. They suggest that the survivor is doing something wrong, rather than that the perpetrator is at fault. There are many reasons people stay in an abusive relationship.

THE HEALING IN SHARING PODCAST EPISODES:

Domestic Violence/Gail Talks About the Honeymoon Stage and Beyond
https://www.buzzsprout.com/1771834/8858305

Bill Lost His Daughter to Dating Violence
https: //www.buzzsprout.com/1771834/9552710

Ryan, A Male Survivor of Domestic Violence
https://www.buzzsprout.com/1771834/9702437

Kristen's Story: A Cautionary Tale of Online Dating, Assault, and Rape
https://www.buzzsprout.com/1771834/10856473

GOD DOESN'T
GIVE YOU
anything
YOU CAN'T
handle

STORY 2

SURVIVING ARMED ROBBERY & ABDUCTION

FEBRUARY 2012

I worked as a store manager at a women's clothing store. I loved helping women find the perfect outfit that made them feel special inside and out. I enjoyed building relationships and turning customers into repeat shoppers. The store was like a second home to me, and I worked many hours to make it successful and to build a team loyal to the brand and to our clients. As a chain clothing store, it had several locations, but I wanted shoppers to think of our location as their number-one shopping destination.

I became the brand media spokesperson for the local market. I appeared on the local CBS station multiple times to discuss fashion and how our brand meets your professional, travel, and everyday needs. In July 2011, that role led the company to select me to participate in a media spokesperson training day in New York, where they also surprised us with tickets to the Broadway show *Mamma Mia*! It was fun and a truly one-of-a-kind experience. I loved my job and the recognition I received.

In February 2012, I received a call from my district manager. One of our stores, about twenty miles north, had been robbed! The news rattled the district, and precautionary plans were put in place. Our stores weren't equipped with security cameras, so they assigned security personnel to each store, and Loss Prevention led a mandatory conference call with all store managers. The call was informative, and we discussed what to do if you are being robbed. I remembered a few takeaways: You don't want to startle the robber or make him nervous, so keep your movements subtle. Remember what you can about the robber's appearance: clothes, tattoos, etc. I listened and shared the information with the rest of my staff. I found the information helpful and tucked it away, thinking I would never need it.

The robbers hit twelve women-owned businesses in total before the robberies stopped in mid-February. They were all located farther north. Security was called in to our stores, and everything was back to normal.

2 MONTHS LATER

My district manager came to visit on a Tuesday. Spring and Easter were our peak sales periods, so we discussed the floor layout, inventory, and staffing needs for those periods. While standing next to me, my manager received a call; the robberies were starting up again. She asked me if I felt safe. The other robberies had occurred twenty miles north of where we were, so I told her I did. I had no reason to think he would come our way.

My store was in a strip center: Target and Best Buy were on the ends, with multiple stores in between. The center was busy, especially on weekends. It was close to the highway, hotels, and a movie theater. In my naïve mind, I would never have considered such a location desirable for committing a robbery.

I worked most weekends because it was the busiest time of the week for sales. On this particular Saturday, one sales associate and I were working the closing shift. It was typical to have only two employees working. It was busy, with me helping five people in the fitting rooms, the sales associate ringing up a customer's purchase, and a husband walking around the sales floor, patiently waiting for his wife to find a dress so they could leave.

A mom and two young boys were seated on a bench in one fitting room while I was helping a grandmother and granddaughter find a dress for their special occasion. The building's layout meant that when I was helping customers outside the fitting rooms, I couldn't see who was entering or exiting the store.

A voice behind me

I remember looking at the mom when someone behind me suddenly shouted, "Give me all your money!" I stood there, processing what I'd heard; it wasn't the usual "Can you zip me up? Do you have matching jewelry?"

I didn't turn around. I just stood there. Again, I heard "Give me all your money!" After hearing the demand twice, I turned to see a masked man pointing a gun at me. I looked at the gun, close enough that I could touch it. I looked at the robber's face, then back at the gun. Then I turned and started toward the register area. My sales associate stared at me as I walked toward her. Out of the corner of my eye, I saw the robber wave the gun, signaling the other people in the store to follow my lead.

As I walked to the register, I wondered how long he had been watching me before he realized I was the one he needed to reach. How long had he been in the store? Days? Hours? Or was this just a spur-of-the-moment decision? The sales associate stepped aside so I could get behind the register.

The words from my conference call kept ringing in my head. "Say as little as possible, try to remember what he looks like." The man ordered the other customers to line up in front of the cash wrap area. They were standing to my right, and the robber was in front of me, pointing the gun at them. He asked for their wallets and any money they had. I opened the first register and gave him the cash. To avoid speaking and risking startling the robber, I used my hand to move it across the till where the coins were held. It was my way of asking him without speaking, "Do you want the loose coins too?"

He said, "No." I set the almost-empty till on the counter and went to the other register.

As I stood closer to the customers, I heard crying. The male customer was praying, "Our Father who art in heaven . . ."

"Shhh," another customer tried to quiet the praying. She was worried it might upset the robber. I could see the panic and fear in the people around me.

I emptied the other register of cash and handed it to the robber. He wore latex gloves and put the loot in a bag. I left the till on the counter. Pointing the gun at me, he asked, "Where is your safe?"

I said, "We don't have one."

Again, he asked, "Where's your safe?"

"We don't have one." It was concerning that he had asked again. I was concerned he didn't believe me, and I wondered what he would do to me or us if he thought I was lying.

Why is he still here?

He stole our money and was still in the store. I knew this was going a little differently from the other robberies, assuming it was the same robber. Previously, he'd taken the cash and left.

Why was he still there? He saw the white swinging door behind me.

“What is that?” he asked.

“That’s the door leading to the stockroom and my office.”

He waved his gun and said, “OK, I want you to go back there.”

He had our money; the clock was ticking, and the longer he stayed in the store, the greater the chance he would be noticed or remembered by the nine witnesses. I didn’t know what else he wanted. He waved the gun, and I ushered everyone to go in front of me. I wanted to be the last in this procession. Several things happened in that moment. I can best describe it as an out-of-body experience. I became unaware that I was a mom, a daughter, a friend, an aunt, etc. These strangers, these customers, had now become my kids. They became my family, and more than anything, I felt an intense need to protect them. I urged them to go first. If he was going to hurt someone, I wanted it to be me; I needed it to be me! I needed to protect them, no matter what.

The sales associate pushed open the doors, and each person made their way into the backroom one at a time. Before I could reach them, he stopped me again.

“Where’s your safe?” he asked.

Again, I explained to him that we didn’t have a safe, which was true. We passed by the back door. He asked me whether it was locked.

I said, "It should be, and if you push on it, it's going to set off an alarm."

We were all reunited in our back stockroom, lined up in front of my desk. He asked me to pull the landline out of the wall and told us to give him our cell phones. I watched the customers hand over their phones from their purses or pockets. While they were doing this, he asked me about an enclosed room a few feet from where we were standing.

Our final destination

I told him it was district storage, a place where we kept hangers and fixtures. Instinctively, I knew he was going to make us go into that room. I also knew I hadn't given him my cell phone, which was still in my pants pocket. I quickly realized that the outline of my cell phone would show through my pocket if I turned to walk into that room. So I gave him my phone, just like the others had, and I was left with no landline and no cell phone.

My instincts were right. The man told us to go into the room. I went after the other customers and the sales associate, and he followed me in. I was leaning against the back wall, my bottom resting on a box of hangers, leaving an indentation in the cardboard, with the others to my left. The robber asked me an unusual question about the door to this room. He wanted to know whether the door shut.

I answered him, "We've never shut that door, but I would assume it closes."

By then, the scenery had changed, but the crying, the praying, and the sounds of a mother consoling her children could still be heard. He looked at us, pointed the gun, and said, "Don't say anything, and nobody will get hurt."

He went to the door, keeping his eyes on us and still pointing the gun. He repeated, "Don't say anything, and nobody will get hurt." He pulled the door shut. You could hear the scrape of wood.

The nine of us sat there in shock. One minute we were simply going about our business on a busy Saturday afternoon, and the next we were being held hostage in a storage room.

The doorbell rang

It was semi-dark as I took in the scene around me. I noticed the grandmother beginning to gasp for air. She was starting to panic. I rushed over to her as her granddaughter, visibly shaken, backed away. I braced the grandmother's arms against the wall and looked straight into her eyes. "I need you to stay with me. I need you to breathe." I began to regulate my breathing, slowly in and out, for her to follow. I was losing the battle.

I could feel her body start to sink as she was no longer able to hold herself up. I called the male customer over and, in a rush, told him I needed his help to keep her from falling. With his help, we safely got her to the floor.

As a store manager, I was often in the store by myself. I was trained to listen for the front doorbell while working in the stockroom. It would alert me when someone entered or exited the store. At that moment, while the grandmother was on the floor, I heard the doorbell ring and hoped it meant the robber had left.

But immediately, my attention returned to the grandmother. Her panic was worsening. If you've ever seen someone have a panic attack, it looks like they can't catch their breath. It's a helpless moment not only for the person experiencing it but also for anyone trying to help.

Then, lightning-fast, she got worse. One moment, a panic attack, and the next, the grandmother was having a full-fledged seizure. I know how to put on a Band-Aid, and that is the extent of my medical experience.

This was the moment panic set in for me. I remember thinking, "If she dies, I might as well admit myself to the hospital because I won't be OK." But I swallowed the panic. I had no other choice, and when I did, I heard the doorbell again. Had someone left or entered the store? Did the robber come back? This was not good! Everything seemed to be happening at once.

Was the robber coming back?

I was praying the robber had left, but I wasn't sure. Just then, the sales associate pulled her cell phone from inside her bra. She had hidden it. I told her to call 911 and to get behind me so she would be somewhat hidden. If the robber came back and pushed open the door, I didn't want him catching her on the phone. She hid and gave the 911 operator her location and the details they asked for. But then I heard the doorbell again and didn't know who was in the store. So I told her to hang up, sit down, turn off the ringer, and put the phone away.

After she hung up, I heard the doorbell again. I had no idea what was going on outside the door. Everyone in the room shifted to the left. I was sitting on the floor next to the grandmother's head, listening to customers' suggestions for how to help her. But nothing made sense. I was way out of my league, and I didn't want to try something and end up hurting her.

She was getting worse by the minute. I looked at my sales associate and said, "Give me your phone. I must call 911." At that point, I knew the grandmother needed help soon, and I was willing to risk the robber's wrath if he opened the door and caught me on the phone.

The 9-1-1 call

The female dispatcher heard my frantic voice and had only a limited description of what was going on. Once I told her I had a customer who was having a seizure and that I needed her help because I didn't know what I was doing, she gave me step-by-step instructions on how to help. She was patient and kind, and to this day, I have the utmost respect for 911 operators.

The door pushed open!

I was on the phone with dispatch when we heard the sound of scraping wood again. The door was suddenly pushed open. I was terrified. Was it the robber coming back?

I looked up from my seated position on the floor to discover it was law enforcement. In that moment, the emotions ran rampant. You could hear everybody take a breath, all sharing the same sense of relief. We knew we were safe and protected.

The paramedics arrived and immediately began assisting the woman who was having a seizure. They ushered the other customers out of the room and instructed them to sit in the shoe department. The police questioned them about all the details they remembered.

In the midst of it all, an officer looked at me and said, "You look relatively calm given everything that just happened."

"Give me a couple of hours, and I'm not going to be OK," I said. "Right now, I need a cigarette."

Catching the robber

Finally, it was my turn to show the police officers my identification. I walked over to my desk. I knew my red wallet had been there. I shuffled through papers and looked on the floor. It had to be there. It held my credit cards, my ID with my current address, and all the usual documents I carry. I stopped and had to accept that my wallet wasn't there. Now I had no phone and no wallet.

The police officers informed me that when they entered the store, they found customers shopping even though no employees were present and the register tills, empty of bills, were lying on the counter. The police had ushered the customers out and then continued their search for us.

Seeing the blue lights flashing and the yellow "Do Not Cross" tape outside our front doors, I felt a little shaken. It was like a scene from a movie, but for me it was real. I was on autopilot. I remember pulling out the white binder with important contact numbers and calling my district manager, giving details I could recall in the moment. I could feel the adrenaline start to subside, and the anxiety kick in. My body started to shake. "Not now!" I told myself.

The officers went outside to search the trash for my phone and wallet. Nothing. During this time, I remembered I had the

"Where's My Droid" app on my phone. I told the officers they could track my phone, and they did.

I stayed with a friend that night and tried to drink until I was numb, and the shaking would stop. I cried all night and couldn't sleep.

The next morning, Sunday, the memories of what had happened the night before came flooding back, stronger than ever. I put on sunglasses to hide my red, puffy, unrecognizable eyes. My friend dropped me off at the store, still considered a crime scene. Everything was a blur. I met the police officers so we could walk the scene while I tried to remember everything I could. They wanted me to think about people I'd seen in the store earlier that day and anyone who resembled the robber or was wearing clothes like his. By late morning, I was headed home, exhausted.

About 4:30 a.m. the next Monday, I received a call from the detective. He apologized for waking me up but said he felt I would want to know what he was about to tell me. They pinged my phone and located the robber and the driver. They arrested both men! Luckily, the robber had kept my phone rather than discarding it as evidence of his crime.

That same day, my district and regional managers came to town. We went to lunch at Applebee's to discuss everything, including me and how I was doing. My district manager filed workers' comp paperwork for me, and I was placed on a ten-day leave from work. Upper management seemed very concerned and accommodating of my needs.

After catching the robber and the getaway car driver, I spent almost every day that week with the detective and police officers, helping them build a solid case by providing as many details as I could. Helping them and being in their presence made me feel safe.

They recognized that the recollections were taking a toll on me. I cried a lot, and they strongly encouraged me to seek professional help. They offered to find help for me if I needed it.

It's OK to ask for help

I decided to start therapy as my ten days of leave were nearing an end. I cried a lot during the sessions. What seemed to haunt me about this traumatic situation was confronting the realities of what *could* have happened. I knew what happened. I had lived to share the story, but my mind kept wandering to hypotheticals like what if the lady had died, what if he raped me in the bathroom, what if this, what if that.

I struggled with having my sense of safety shattered, too. Feeling safe is something we take for granted. Previously, I'd felt safe in the store. As I said, it had been a second home for me. I spent many hours alone there, working on shipments, handling schedules, or catching up. I never worried about anyone violating my safe space. This shattering of my safety extended beyond the store; it seeped into my home environment, too. He'd stolen my wallet, which contained my current address, so he knew where I lived, alone. He'd kept my phone, so I assumed my wallet was in his possession, too. Since my items were never recovered, even though he was arrested, I worried someone else had them and would try to find me.

I took various measures to try to re-establish a sense of safety. The first week after returning to my house, I had a male neighbor stay with me. I had two cats who, fortunately, didn't like strangers, so when I returned home, I wouldn't enter if they weren't on the other side of the door waiting for me. I also put a sliver of paper in the door jamb at the bottom of each door so it wouldn't be noticed. If that piece of paper had fallen to the ground, I knew someone had opened my door and was presumably still inside. I had a front door and a side door, so each door had that little sliver of paper. This became my new normal.

When my ten days of leave were up, the therapist insisted I wasn't ready to return to work.

I'm stubborn and the type of person who doesn't go halfway down a road just to turn around and spend the rest of my life wondering "what if." I must reach the stop sign and know whether I can or not. I needed to go back to work!

Returning to work

Only ten days after the crime, I walked back into my store. I was looking forward to seeing everyone. I had a smile on my face, but deep down I felt fear. I went through the swinging back door, rounded the corner, passed the back exit, and stared into the room where we had been held hostage. I started to shake. It felt like flashbulbs were going off. I could feel all the triggers and see everything I'd remembered. I could not go into that room, our final destination. I stood in its doorway, remembering the crying, praying, and panicking, the sound of doorbells from inside, and the sound of scraping wood. I recalled the feeling of relief when law enforcement rescued us. I backed away from the doorway, never to enter that room again.

After an hour, I joined a conference call. My district manager asked how I was doing, and I told her I didn't think I was OK. Her response was, "This is the busiest time of year for us. If you can't do this, I need to know so I can replace you."

Replaced

From a business perspective, I completely understood. From the compassionate human side, I struggled with this comment because I was an accomplished, respected manager. I delivered results, and they knew it. The realization that I couldn't perform at a high level anymore left me feeling weak and inadequate. While grappling with those feelings, I also thought, "I helped potentially save people's lives, and this is what I get in return?"

The conference call ended, and I needed to go back out onto the sales floor. I pushed open the swinging door and looked straight into the eyes of a man who looked like the robber. To my right was my assistant manager. I grabbed her arm and was about to burst into tears. She said, "What's wrong with you? Are you okay?"

I said, "No! This is what happens to me!" I felt anxious, and my body started to shake. The man standing there apologized, saying he didn't mean to scare me. It turned out he was our security guard, but it didn't matter because he'd triggered a memory of the robber. I looked at him and said, "It's not you. It's me. I'm so sorry!" If ever that relationship line was true, it was in that moment. I was embarrassed and humiliated. I'm not afraid of men, but the situation triggered fear in me.

I knew I wasn't OK. I could barely stand to be in our stockroom. This reaction was the final straw, and I realized I couldn't do the job. I couldn't be there anymore, and I needed to get better. I called my district manager, told her what happened, and said I couldn't do the job anymore. I was going to be replaced.

I gathered my belongings, said goodbye to the staff, and apologized to the security guard once more as I left the store. I continued my therapy sessions and lived off workman's comp for six more weeks.

For months after the robbery, I had a stack of subpoenas summoning me to court for motions and pretrial hearings.

The first jury trial

Recalling how soon after the robbery this event occurred is difficult. I estimate it was less than nine months. The first time I saw the getaway car driver was in court. When I walked into the courtroom, I was caught off guard to see that the "accomplice" had friends and/or family there. I felt a new fear. What were these people thinking? Were they going to follow me? Did they want to hurt me? They knew what I looked like. They knew what I drove. Were they going to follow me home? When court was over, I took a new route home.

Testifying before a jury was emotionally exhausting. I presume the jury needed to see what his actions, as the accomplice, had done to me. He contributed to my trauma, which still felt fresh in my mind.

I ended up finding a new job in the same industry and continued attending any court hearings that were scheduled. The robber was charged with multiple felonies, including the use of a firearm, wearing a mask in public, robbery, possession of a firearm by a convicted felon, larceny, and nine counts of abduction. There was enough evidence; it didn't go to trial. It wasn't quite a year, and the court summons were over, so I could close this chapter. I decided to move north and "start over."

NOVEMBER 2014

The appeal

Two and a half years after the robbery, I received a voicemail from an unfamiliar number. I listened as a woman said, "I'm going to need you to come to federal court to testify in a jury trial." I called her back and told her I couldn't do it. "You don't understand," I pleaded. She told me the robber had appealed, and I had no choice but to be there.

I hung up the phone and cried. All the emotions, the fear, everything, came flooding back. Everything I'd worked so hard to deal with and heal from was exposed as a raw wound again. Regular court was bad enough, but when you hear the words "federal court," you automatically sense the seriousness.

The appeal was based on a couple of things, one of which was a lack of sufficient evidence. There were two eyewitnesses, one of whom was me. I had seen the robber's mustache through the mask, the whites of his eyes bulging, and that he was dark-skinned. One of the eyewitnesses observed the robber before he pulled the mask over his face.

I drove an hour and a half to the courthouse and was ushered into a room with a long table and many chairs. The other survivors from that day had also been summoned, and it was the first time I'd seen them since.

Thank you

I sat at the table, looked at everyone seated with me, and said, "Thank you. Thank you for trusting me enough to follow my lead." You don't know how you'll respond to situations like this. One of them could have wanted to be a hero, reacted radically, and startled the robber, drastically changing the outcome. I was thankful for the opportunity to express my thanks to them.

A lady dressed in a suit entered the room. She asked for our contact information because they wanted to reimburse us for our mileage and gas. When it was my turn to provide my information, I looked at the lady and said, "I don't want your money. I just want you to leave me alone."

The tears began to come.

She said, "I'm sorry. We want to help you this way." I reiterated that I just wanted to be left alone and didn't want any money. Nevertheless, months later, I received a check in the mail for about $400.00.

My turn to testify

I waited nervously for my turn to testify. This courtroom was different; it was larger, with more people, and filled with chairs and pews made of dark wood. I remember walking down the aisle, staring straight ahead, and entering the booth where I was to be seated for the trial. The booth was to the right of the judge, and the robber was in front of me. This time, he was wearing glasses. It was the first time I'd seen him since the night of the robbery.

The attorneys asked me a series of questions, and as I continued to tell my story, I cried. They brought me water and some Kleenex. By the time I finished for the day, the Kleenex had become a wet ball in my hand, crumbling into little pieces, which was exactly how I felt inside.

I had to return the next day and was scheduled to testify first. When we finished, the judge looked at me and asked, "Do you have any questions?"

"Yes. Do I ever have to come back?" I asked.

The judge replied, "No, ma'am, you will not have to come back."

I looked at him with relief and said, "Thank you."

I have not had to return to court, and the robber is still in prison.

The chapter on the robbery is closed!

Triggers

I was left with a noticeable trigger: I don't like being called from behind me. Four years after the robbery, when my husband and I first started dating, he would speak to me from behind, and it would startle me. Instantly, from the top of my head to the bottom of my toes, I felt fear followed by anger. I would turn around, trying to control the strong adverse emotions before speaking to him. "Please don't call me from behind. It startles me, and then I get scared and angry." Now, ten years after the robbery, my startle response is still sensitive but calming.

Nine years later

Many years after the ordeal, I discovered a hidden trigger. To give you some background, I grew up in a family of hunters. I was surrounded by rifles and handguns, and I took archery and hunter safety classes. I never feared guns. In fact, even as a survivor of gun violence, I blame the person holding the gun, not the gun.

My husband asked if I would like to take concealed carry classes, but the thought of seeing a gun close enough to touch petrified me. I would start shaking. Realizing something wasn't right about this reaction, I decided I didn't want this fear to control me. I wasn't going to allow this device, which instilled fear in me, to control me. I was going to control it. Through private lessons with an awesome trainer (Freddie at Frogbones Family Shooting Center), I learned to properly handle and use a gun. I have a healthy fear and respect for a gun, which I use solely for protection.

Why I Survived

Almost a decade after the armed robbery, I realized it was time to tell the world what had happened. I watched violence in our country escalate and our first responders' courageous acts receive only dim spotlighting. I felt called to find my inner courage, share my story, and remind others they're not alone. I was also called to give thanks to all the first responders who helped me that day and who help strangers every day.

Every day, people like me who are thrust into traumatic situations need space to share their experiences in a nonjudgmental, compassionate environment. The journey from victim to survivor is transformative and varied. No two stories are the same, and each path to healing is unique. Together, we share to create awareness, heal, and educate, so others can hopefully prevent themselves from becoming victims too.

THE HEALING IN SHARING PODCAST EPISODES:

S1 Ep 1 – Surviving Armed Robbery & Abduction (Jen's story Pt 1)
https://www.buzzsprout.com/1771834/8500288

S1 Ep 2 – Surviving Armed Robbery & Abduction (Jen's story Pt 2) Featuring Alan P. Smith, Licensed Clinical Social Work/Therapist
https://www.buzzsprout.com/1771834/8562299

NEVER APOLOGIZE TO *anyone* FOR TRUSTING YOUR GUT

STORY 3

I SURVIVED "CREEPY GUY"

(SITUATIONAL AWARENESS)

APRIL 2022

I was headed to a work conference. By then, I had been podcasting for about a year and was excited to be surrounded by my peers and experts in the field and to take advantage of an incredible networking opportunity. I planned to travel there alone.

MAY 19TH

A week before heading to the conference, a mutual acquaintance introduced me to a guy named Matt, who was also going to attend the event. We had friendly phone chats and planned to meet there. I felt reassured knowing someone would be there.

MAY 26TH

Thursday morning, I was packed and headed out the door at 6:00 a.m. I left my computer at home; there would be no time for emails, just networking and making new friends. I checked in to the event and received a lanyard with my name on it. The energy was buzzing and fun, and it was exciting to be there.

After lunch, I attended a track featuring female entrepreneurs. During a break, a man approached me and asked what my podcast was about.

"I'm a survivor of armed robbery and abduction, and I started my podcast to create a space where survivors of traumatic events can share their stories. I focus on topics that are uncomfortable to discuss: domestic violence, human trafficking, fentanyl, the foster care system, etc. I partner with local, national, and international organizations that provide resources for trauma survivors. In addition, I spotlight the unique traumas our first responders face," I replied.

I asked him the same question. As he spoke, I listened and observed him. "I interview people. who . . ." His words were drowning out as I felt something wasn't right. My instincts were telling me to pay attention. He finished speaking and asked if he could take our picture. "Sure," I said. We exchanged business cards and headed off in our own directions, the something-isn't-right feeling lingering after he walked away.

I wanted to focus on learning and having fun, so I dismissed the feeling, telling myself, "He's probably a nice guy. Stop being paranoid." Still, something about it felt kind of creepy.

MAY 27TH

On Friday, I met Matt for lunch in a large conference room while listening to a keynote speaker. It was great to finally meet after our phone conversations. We enjoyed pizza, chatted, and then headed to different tracks. We planned to meet up for a happy hour later in the evening.

During the afternoon, as I was walking through the conference halls, I kept noticing Creepy Guy from the day before. On occasion, he'd say, "Hi, Jen." His presence always set off red flags, and I was beginning to take my feelings more seriously.

Matt and I met for the happy hour, and as we sat at a round table, chatting about our exciting day and all we'd learned, Creepy Guy walked in. He stopped at the entrance, quickly looked to his right and left, then looked straight ahead and locked eyes with me. He headed to our table, pulled a chair out, sat down, looked at me, and said, "Hi, Jen!" I said hi back, but my stomach was churning. There were several tables and empty chairs, yet he sat in front of me at the same table.

A minute later, Creepy Guy was up and mingling with others.

I observed Matt watching Creepy Guy speak with two women. As they responded to his questions, he looked these ladies up and down. I looked at Matt and asked what he thought. Matt agreed that there was something not quite right about him. I felt better when Matt confirmed my thoughts and feelings. I wasn't alone in my "judgment."

MAY 28TH

Saturday morning, Matt and I walked the halls of the conference center, burning off some breakfast calories. We passed Creepy Guy as he headed in the opposite direction. At that point, I walked past him with my head down, not wanting to acknowledge him. "He watched you the whole time as he passed us," Matt said. I told Matt he creeped me out and that I was going home. My husband and I had plans that evening anyway. Since we passed Creepy Guy going the other way, I figured I didn't have to worry about seeing him again.

I said goodbye to Matt and walked toward the lobby. The parking garage was beneath the hotel, and you had to take an outdoor elevator at the back of the hotel. As I passed the registration desk, I looked to my left and saw Creepy Guy standing with his back to me. Immediately, I wondered how he had slipped past us without our noticing.

My heart beat a little faster as I put my head down and picked up my pace. I turned a corner and found myself in front of two sets of elevators. Two women joined me as I waited, and the three of us got on the elevator when it arrived. As the doors began to close, I let out a deep breath, realizing how nervous that last encounter with Creepy Guy had made me. My phone was in my hand, and I looked down at it as the doors started closing. Suddenly, I saw feet! It was like watching a horror movie. One minute, nobody, and the next second, boom! There were feet. I looked up, and my eyes must have looked like they were about to pop out of their sockets. Standing there was Creepy Guy, pushing the elevator doors open. He was facing us, each arm pushing the corresponding door. When the doors were open enough, he turned sideways and made his way in, freeing his backpack, which was momentarily stuck in the doorway, by shifting his body to make it fit.

There we were in the elevator: Creepy Guy and me, with two women between us. He glared at me and asked, "Did you have a restful evening, Jen?" Pause.

"Yes," I replied. I asked him, "Are you leaving?" He stuttered, as though he hadn't expected the question. "I'm going to my car to get water because I'm parched."

Everything in me went off. All the red flags were raised and flying so furiously in front of me that you would have thought hurricane winds had entered the elevator. We had just left a hotel with free, cold water, and he was going to his hot car to get water? No. This was not a good situation! I knew I couldn't get off the elevator when the doors opened. I knew I couldn't go anywhere with him.

My sense of safety was shaken. This feeling was all too familiar as triggers from the robbery a decade ago flooded my mind and body. I had to keep it together! Now was not the time to panic! But what could I do?

The elevator doors opened, and the women stepped out. Creepy Guy stepped out, turned around, and waited for me to exit the elevator as well. I looked down at my phone and said, "I must go back. I forgot something." I didn't move, and slowly the doors closed. When I didn't get off the elevator, I heard a loud grunt from the man. It was a sound of agitation, disappointment, frustration, and anger.

The elevator doors closed, and I texted Matt to let him know I was on my way back up and needed him to walk me to my car. After I explained what happened, Matt said he would report the man to the venue after walking me to my car. As we walked through the lobby, Creepy Guy appeared, heading our way. My friend pushed me behind a wide pillar, hiding me; Creepy Guy couldn't see me.

Matt watched as the man stopped on the other side of the pillar where I was hiding and checked his phone. That made me suspect he was tracking me. He turned right, headed to the drinking fountain, and began drinking. Matt pulled on my shoulder and said, "Come on. We need to go."

We continued along the familiar path I had taken just minutes earlier. With our pace brisk and my heart pounding, I was afraid to look back to see if he was following us. We reached the elevators, pushed the button, and waited. The doors opened, and we stepped in. I watched closely, praying I wouldn't see feet again. When we reached the basement, I hopped off first, followed by Matt. As we headed to my car, we both looked back to make sure we weren't being followed. We found my car, and I loaded my luggage. I couldn't see the elevator, but Matt could watch for anyone getting off.

I was visibly shaken by the encounter. Matt looked over at me and said, "I had no idea what it was like for you, as a woman, to always have to be aware of your surroundings." His tone was full of concern and empathy.

I replied, "Yes. Always!" with my voice shaking.

With no sign of Creepy Guy, I said goodbye to Matt and thanked him for helping me. I got in my car, locked the doors, and backed out of my parking spot. As I left the garage, I saw Matt watching to make sure I could leave safely. I headed home.

On the way, I called my husband to tell him what happened. My ride home felt long, with many thoughts filling my head. "I don't want to feel this fear for my safety again. Even so, I'm stronger now. I don't want to cry. But I do want to cry. I should call the police. I don't need to call the police. Let me just push this feeling way down and pretend I'm not scared right now. I'll put a smile on my face and be thankful nothing happened."

I made it home and hugged my husband. We agreed I wouldn't travel alone again. As I headed to unpack my suitcase, I told him I needed to forget it had happened.

Shortly after, I checked my phone to turn off location services. I went through Instagram and Facebook to block him wherever I could. I saved his picture on my phone, too. I tried to write it off as a bad situation and tell myself I was fine, that I was safe.

But by the next night, I wasn't OK. I walked into the living room and told my husband I needed a hug, but that he couldn't ask me any questions. As he embraced me, the tears started to flow. He asked what was wrong, and I explained that Creepy Guy had really scared me.

My husband got upset, and I could hear the frustration in his voice as he assured me, once again, that he'd go with me next time. We hugged each other, and he felt helpless.

My husband encouraged me to report the incident to law enforcement, but I wasn't sure I wanted to. Matt reported the incident to the venue, and they said they would include it in the debrief. As my fear began to subside, I felt guilt. "What if he hurts someone else, and I didn't say anything to prevent it?" I felt like a hypocrite. My goal is to help people. I encourage people to ask for help, yet I hadn't!

It's amazing what emotions and thoughts go through one's head after a traumatic experience. My body was going through so many things that I wasn't able to process much beyond what was happening in the moment. I finally remembered that I should be gentle with myself.

MAY 30TH

On Monday, I called the local county sheriff's department. No crime was committed, but they took the information and gave me an incident number. I was told to be aware of my surroundings and to call my local sheriff's department if he showed up anywhere I was. It was a positive interaction, and I'm glad I called. I have not seen Creepy Guy since.

The chapter of Creepy Guy is closed.

THE HEALING IN SHARING PODCAST EPISODE:

Pam escaped "Creepy Guy"/ Situational Awareness with Mike Dandridge
https://www.buzzsprout.com/1771834/11128136

BY REPLACING "FEAR" WITH "*faith*" WE CAN FULFILL OUR *purpose*

STORY 4

"INTENTION" VS. "PURPOSE" —AN INSPIRING MOMENT AT THE BEACH

OCTOBER 11, 2007

I awoke this Saturday morning with the idea of going to the beach. As strong as the urge to go was, there was an equally strong urge not to go. I thought about the two-hour one-way drive, the cost of gas, the chilly temperatures, and the chores I could finish at home. My mind was full of objections, but the urge to go was stronger.

After an hour-long debate with myself, I decided to go, sit on the beach, and write. I love writing, and it proved to be cheap therapy. I gathered everything I would need and headed out. It was cloudy, but hopefully the sun would be shining at the beach.

It was an easy drive, and since it was off-season, parking was easy to find. I joined four other cars in the "free parking" lot. I opened my car door and instantly felt the cool wind. Not a breeze, but wind. As the air whipped my hair and hit my face, I thought maybe this wasn't such a good idea. I pulled out my spare coat from the backseat and put it on. I grabbed my bag and headed toward the boardwalk. I could see the sand and hear the furious roar of the waves.

I walked the boardwalk, heading south so the wind was at my back. The sky was a light blue, with clouds scattered about and the sun peeking through where it could. I could feel the wind on my back; my T-shirt, turtleneck, and fleece pullover absorbed it before it reached my skin. I carried my black bag over my shoulder.

I had been to the beach on two other occasions, but this time was different. The scenery and the people were different. I didn't see tourists or locals walking about, but rather a handful of homeless people asleep on benches, covered in whatever they could find to stay warm. Others were gathered, talking among themselves.

As I became more aware of my surroundings, I grew afraid. I was here by myself, and I hadn't let anyone know I was leaving town. As I walked, I glanced over my shoulder to see if I had been followed and listened for footsteps. I walked a little farther, then decided to head back the way I came. I was headed toward the homeless people again.

I passed a man asleep on a bench. His red, chapped hands lay folded on his chest. They were in desperate need of warmth. His backpack lay on the ground. As I walked by, I wanted to give him one of my blankets, but I was afraid he would attack me. I was honestly afraid. I lived a sheltered life, rarely exposed to homelessness or homeless people. I knew what I saw on TV or heard from others. Some stories were good, and others not so good. I wasn't looking to find out what kind of story these homeless people would leave me with.

I walked toward the sand. I took off my shoes, but the sand was cold and unwelcoming. When I pulled out my blanket, the wind caught it. I managed to pull it down, and it landed in the sand, disheveled. This was not working out well.

I sat down and pulled out my notebook and pen. My hands were cold, and it was impossible to write with the pen. I looked to my left, down the boardwalk, at the shops and restaurants lining the way. There was a restaurant open with a sign that read, "Fish and Chips." That would work. I gave up on the beach, packed my things back into the bag, and headed toward the restaurant. As I walked, I noticed the homeless people again. I wondered what had happened in their lives to put them where they were.

I arrived at the restaurant entrance, pulled open the door, and was greeted by the warmth inside. I sat at the booth and ordered coffee and fish and chips. I unzipped my coat and felt the artificial heat. My hands and fingers warmed as I held my hot coffee cup.

While waiting for my food, I started talking to God, "I want to help these homeless people, but I'm afraid. Maybe I can take some blankets to a shelter instead?" I pulled out my pen and paper and began writing about this experience. I have my writings from that day, neatly tucked away in a folder. I have nothing written on paper beyond my time in this restaurant because what happened next changed my life forever.

I had half a meal left, which I boxed up and put in a bag. I put on my coat and bundled up, ready to head back out into the wind. It was time to head home. I walked out the front door of the restaurant and stopped for my after-meal cigarette. I looked out at the beach, the boardwalk, and the people walking about. There were more locals out and about, and I didn't feel as alone as I had earlier. I finished my cigarette and walked up the steps onto the boardwalk. As I walked, a homeless man kept his eyes on me and started walking my way. As fear started to set in, I heard a voice inside: "It's OK. He won't hurt you. He just wants a cigarette." Sure enough, the man walked up to me and asked for a cigarette. "Sure," I said as I reached into my bag and pulled out what he asked for. I handed him the cigarette and lit it for him. This was the closest encounter I'd ever had with a homeless person.

I will never forget his hands; they were red and chapped, like the hands of the sleeping man I'd seen earlier. When I looked at his face, it matched his hands. I hated being cold, and I couldn't imagine how he felt. I looked at him and asked if he'd like some blankets. He looked over at a woman lying on the bench and said yes. I took my blankets out of my bag and handed them to him. Then I asked if he'd like some food and offered him my leftovers. His eyes filled with tears. "Yes. Thank you. You are so nice." I handed him the bag with the Styrofoam container of food, gave him another cigarette, and told him to take care of himself. I turned and headed toward the stairs.

During the ride home, I realized something. While I intended to enjoy the beach scenery and write, my true purpose for this trip was to make a small difference in someone else's life by sharing what I already had. I walked away from the man on the boardwalk feeling I'd fulfilled my purpose. I did a good deed, and it required very little from me. I prayed to God for a way to help. I became aware of my surroundings, noticed more people around, and instinctively knew the homeless man wanted a cigarette. In that moment, the elements aligned, so I felt safer and could help. There was a plan for me that day, and I was able to fulfill it. Ever since I was a child, I knew my purpose was to help people. I always said to God, "I will help wherever, whenever, and however you need me to if you guide me there."

God guided me through all these struggles. I had many times where I looked up to heaven and said, "Really? How much more do you think I can take?" But here I am!

My passion and purpose now are to continue my podcast and write more books to help others to share, learn, and grow.

ACKNOWLEDGMENTS

To my husband, Willie, you are amazing, and with you by my side, I can achieve anything. I love you.

To my boys, Kyle and Colin, I love you. You inspire me every day to push my limits. I'm proud of the men you have become. Each day, I look forward to watching you grow and succeed in your life journeys. Together, we will always be the Three Musketeers!

To Naz and Giancarlo, I am grateful for an amazing daughter-in-law and a beautiful grandbaby.

To Marvin, we met through a mutual connection and attended the same event. Thank you for guiding me to safety.

To my parents and family, thank you for your love and support. I love you.

To Don, Betty, and Russell, your compassion, love, and support will always be cherished. You are family. I love you.

To Mike Dandridge, I appreciate your passion and dedication to helping others stay safe. I'm glad to call you a friend.

To Bill Mitchell, host of the *When Dating Hurts* podcast, your courage to share your daughter's story inspired me to share mine.

To Scott Johnson, Host of the *What Was That Like* podcast, I appreciate your time in mentoring me along the way. Your honesty challenged me to be a better podcaster. Thank you!

To my friend Joe, you always said I was destined for greatness. Thank you for believing in me.

To my friends and podcast guests, you inspire me to keep this journey going. It is because of you that *The Healing In Shairng* lives today. Your courage, dedication, and commitment to *your* healing journey keep the fire burning inside me. We are "survivor" strong!

To Beacon Point LLC, I would like to thank their editors for their valuable contributions to my book. Their editing polished the content in my story. I recommend them for your publishing projects.

To Lindsey Nolan, Lindsey Nolan Portrait, thank you for capturing my "survivor smile." She is credited for my book cover photos.

To Stephanie Thompson, Thompson Editing, thank you for your contributions to my book.

To Jen Henderson at Wild Words Formatting, thank you for formatting my book so it can be a lifeline for so many.

ABOUT THE AUTHOR

Jennifer Lee is the creator and host of The Healing in Sharing podcast (formerly the I Need Blue podcast), a space for honest conversations about resilience, healing, and the power of sharing our stories. A survivor, storyteller, and community builder, Jennifer believes healing begins when people feel seen, heard, and understood.

Her work is rooted in lived experience. Through her writing, speaking, and podcasting, she creates space for vulnerability without shame and for strength without perfection. Jennifer's storytelling invites readers and listeners to reflect on their journeys, honor their scars, and recognize the courage it takes to keep going even when the path is unclear.

She is also an advocate for community, frequently collaborating with local organizations, first responders, and mission-driven partners to amplify voices that deserve to be heard. Whether on the page, behind the microphone, or on stage, her message is consistent: you are not alone, and your story matters.

Jennifer is married, a proud mom of two sons who serve in the United States Marine Corps, and a grateful grandmother. She lives in Florida and continues to believe in the quiet power of honesty, compassion, and shared humanity. As she reminds every reader and listener, *you are stronger than you think*.

STAY IN TOUCH

We are the strength for others when they are weak.
We are the ear when they need someone to listen.
We are the voice whispering, "You got this!"

LEARN MORE ABOUT JEN'S JOURNEY

TheHealingInSharing.com

THE *HEALING IN SHARING PODCAST* SERIES

is on most popular listening platforms, including Apple Podcast, Spotify, YouTube, etc.

INSTAGRAM

@thehealinginsharing

YOUTUBE

@ineedblue
@thehealinginsharing11

FACEBOOK

@thehealinginsharing

QUESTIONS OR COMMENTS

Email: TheHealingInSharing@gmail.com

www.ingramcontent.com/pod-product-compliance
Lightning Source LLC
LaVergne TN
LVHW020638100826
845148LV00012B/2230

9798987332146